Substantial Ghosts

Doreen Hinchliffe

Oversteps Books

To Fiona,

with love and thanks.

Doreen Hinchliffe.

First published in 2020 by   Oversteps Books Ltd
                                  6 Halwell House
                                  South Pool
                                  Nr Kingsbridge
                                  Devon
                                  TQ7 2RX
                                  UK

www.overstepsbooks.com

Printed in Great Britain by imprint digital, Devon

In memory of
Sam and Eric

Acknowledgements

Some of these poems, or earlier versions of them, have appeared in the following publications:

Acumen, Artemis, The Cannon's Mouth, Dream Catcher, Live Canon Poetry Competition Anthologies 2009 and 2013, Norwich Poetry Competition Anthology 2007, Orbis, Poetry Life, Reach Poetry, Sentinel Literary Quarterly, Sofia, SOUTH, South Bank Poetry, The Interpreter's House, Ver Poetry Competition Anthology 2018, Ware Poetry Competition Anthology 2011.

The Pointing Star sonnet sequence was recorded by Live Canon on their *Poems For Christmas* CD. It was also included in the Christmas anthology, *A Star In The Heart,* edited by David Grubb, 2014.

Thirteen Ways Of Looking at a Snowfall was published in Live Canon's *More Poems For Christmas* anthology, December 2018.

Sea Raven appeared in *For The Silent*, an anthology published in 2019 by Indigo Dreams to raise funds for The League Against Cruel Sports.

I would like to thank the following people for their help in the compilation of this collection:

Tamar Yoseloff for giving her time so generously and for her much-valued support, advice and encouragement.

The members of Tamar Yoseloff's seminar group, Greenwich Poetry Workshop and Greenwich Stanza for their useful comments and suggestions on a number of these poems.

Kathryn Maris and the members of her Advanced Poetry Workshop for many enlightening discussions and constructive feedback on work in progress.

Lin Jonas for her assistance with proofreading.

Contents

The Art of Getting Lost

Practise the art of getting lost
in the deepest forest, not knowing where
it ends, like the leaf of an oak tossed

on a sudden wind, unaware
of anything except the flight
in dappled sun, the ripples of air,

conscious only of slanting light
through branches, of being borne and held,
indifferent to left or right

to future or to past, propelled
into the heart of now by powers
unfathomed, unseen, deep in the meld

and mould of earth, in its tiny flowers
(bluer than bluebells, whiter than frost)
that lie beyond the counting of hours

and the counting of the cost.

Thirteen Ways of Looking at a Snowfall

1   A midnight thief has stunned the graveyard,
    stealing the names of the dead.

2   The petals of a pink cyclamen
    push through, shocking against the white.

3   A thousand gems ignite the hills,
    sparking the slant light of December sun.

4   A crisp sheet, freshly ironed,
    is stamped with the prints of a blackbird.

5   Children are building statues in the park.
    Snow sits up and begs.

6   The hatless snowman is as bald
    as the world around him.

7   A cat dithers on a doorstep,
    wary of sinking his paw in a new puzzle.

8   Along the leaning trunk of an oak,
    huge doilies have been scattered.

9   The ash has donned a bridal dress;
    its branches bend with the weight of white.

10 Muffled stillness hangs in the air;
    sounds are slowed to semibreves.

11 Dusk falls as mist and settles
    like dust on a blank canvas.

12 Flurries of soft grey moths
    cluster round an orange street lamp.

13 There's no sign of the master builder
    that smoothed the world's rough edges.

Inside the Snow Globe

Snow is falling back to sky, wending
its way from earth to heaven in a flurry
of tiny flakes that flutter from roofs and treetops
like a host of white angels ascending.

Drawn by the pull of the silver scimitar,
they rise in spirals, surging and swirling
higher and higher, every twist and turn
reflected in the light of winter stars.

Upended, we cling to casement windows, press
our faces close to frozen glass.
We hold our breath and blink at space around us,
dizzy with our sudden weightlessness.

Now, if we leapt head-first, careless of fears,
would the fluid air sustain us,
bear us through the spinning dark towards
the distant, half-heard music of the spheres?

Ilkley Moor

I wake to find
the swing of winter's pendulum
has brushed the earth,
trailing snow as far as the eye can see.

Beyond the hills
the clouds are making sculptures
for the white eye of the sun
to hide behind, filter through.

The forecast tells
of a world below zero,
clear skies and Arctic winds,
a frost that will last all day.

I walk the moors,
trek for miles to climb the famous cliffs
that centuries have cut and curved
into the figure of a cow and calf.

Gloved fingers
scratch and scrabble as I clamber up,
touch the initials of endless lives
etched in gritstone rock.

Alone at the top,
I gaze on a new horizon;
in snow each landmark's reassigned,
even the woods assume a different shape.

Road has vanished,
river turned to ice,
dry stone walls and hedgerows merge,
ancient ruts and tracks are lost.

Across the fields
the sheep are huddling close,
seeking warmth
in the setting sun's diagonals.

I can't help thinking
it's the right light for angels,
sudden miracles.
Is now the time to steal away unheard,

or should I wait
for moonrise, nightfall,
the promise of a winter sky
exposed and cold and crammed with stars?

Beyond Kyoto

The long note of a temple bell
strikes the August heat, vibrates
and carries down the spine of the valley.

Stirring from sleep on the lip of a pot,
a silk-red butterfly flaps his wings,
heading for the shade of distant pines.

Sound waves cease. A stillness
settles on the wooded hills and slopes.
Leaves hold their breath in windless air.

Through the haze of an amber dusk,
a host of scents meander – Japanese lily,
sweet osmanthus, noble orchid, lotus flower.

The moon unveils above the mountains.
It spreads a silver balm across the fields,
erasing all the scars of ancient lives.

Persephone

The April roots loosen her cerements
and pull her back to earth, this revenant
we sense, sometimes, rising through the scree
in her tiffany gown of periwinkle blue.
Across the mist of dawn she treads so softly,
scattering lady's mantle, ulster mary,
baby's breath and campanula. Her hair,
the colour of kelp, is wreathed with gillyflowers
and forget-me-nots. It floats in the breeze
as she rounds the cliff, uncovering her face.
She stops awhile to gaze on a cerulean
sky, drink in once more the earth's quotidian
colours, so soon forgotten when they fade
to nothing in the underworld of Hades.

Arachne's Gift

through my window pane I see
a miniature epiphany,

        distracting me

suspended from a slender branch,
it hangs in perfect symmetry,

        attracting me

pale raindrops cling to every thread,
it looks translucent, silvery,

        inviting me

fine skeins festoon the falling dusk
like beads around a Christmas tree,

        delighting me

concentric circles interlace
in subtly crafted filigree,

        impressing me

this delicate net of intricate weave –
who dares disturb the geometry

        obsessing me

no wind or storm can break the spell
of infinite fragility

        that's holding me

motionless, I scarcely breathe,
entangled in the mystery

        enfolding me

from rope once used to hang herself
Arachne spun this tapestry

        now calling me

her voice, as soft as gossamer,
intones, *my gift has set you free,*

        enthralling me.

Arachne was blessed with the gift of spinning, but in remorse at provoking Athene's anger, she hanged herself from a tree. Athene then turned her into a spider and transformed the rope from which she was hanging into a silken thread, allowing her to continue spinning forever.

Sea Raven

on the back of the tallest cliff
a green-eyed cormorant stands alone

beyond the reach of spume and foam
tossed up from sea-splashed rocks

he spreads wet wings   holds them aloft
hangs them out to dry in the gathering wind

the slap and swerve of air bends
and batters the long curve of his neck

as he tilts his head far up   far back
his yellow throat stark against a charcoal sky

like some dark angel robed in black and grey
he views the arc and swell of his world

the sheen on his feathers flecked with gold
in the flickering embers of a winter sun

content   he sinks into quiescence   muses on
deep sea diving and the maundering of hapless fish.

How to Speak to Lions

cautiously
head bowed and cap in hand
not wanting to alarm
with a chunk of finest mutton
tucked appeasingly beneath one arm

respectfully
without an ipod ipad
camcorder or mobile phone
and minus any kind of company
assuring them you're utterly alone

inaudibly
in the softest purr
in a voice as small
as a child's whisper
hardly rippling the air at all

deferentially
on feet of silk
acknowledging their royal station
careful to let them exercise
their right to terminate the conversation

warily
maintaining a safe distance
proceeding at their pace
and pausing often to admire
their silently attentive feline grace

reverently
as if they held
the secrets of the Holy Grail
mindful of the spark behind their eyes
the swish of sacred fire in their tail

To the Kingfisher

Hopkins caught your inscape, how you draw
the sun's fire and flash it back in turquoise-
orange flame, dazzling the air with your poise
and artistry, yet hardly seen before
you disappear. For Eliot, your wing
was an antiphon to light, that point behind
the turning world which none of us can find
by hope, as *hope would be hope for the wrong thing*.
And so, I wait, as I have for years, beside
the river, looking out for you at dusk-fall,
for a blur of blue, the tilt of a head where you hide
in the reeds, praying that you'll break your cover.
I listen for your voice, like a lover,
believing that the readiness is all.

A Kind of Valediction

Thomas Stearns turned up in my dream last night.
He was leaning under a gas lamp in the fog.
In the twilight hour between sleep and waking,
I walked towards him over London Bridge
and together we listened to the sound of the Thames.
It still runs softly, he said, *and yet it has undone so many.*

He took my arm and we moved through deserted streets,
the smog lingering at the back of our throats.
There was no sign of the old pock-marked moon
but we saw a dozen cats rubbing their backs
against the terraced window panes. Whiskers
twitching, they purred and bowed as he passed.

At the end of a long row of cheap one-night hotels,
he pointed to the ledge of a Victorian pub
where window boxes sprouted dead geraniums,
their crooked stalks clawing the air like talons.
Here, we stood for a while, gazing on crazy paving,
inhaling the scent of chestnuts and stale beer.

What is the late November doing? he whispered,
as the withered leaves rustled beneath our feet.
Is it disturbing the dust of your past?
We stopped beside a half-remembered gate
and I heard again the wood thrush of my childhood,
his song rising high above us through the mist.

A silence surrounded us then, the city seeming unreal.
In your beginning is your end, he murmured,
behind his voice the sound of a hidden waterfall.
On Queen Victoria Street, he left me, raising his bowler
in a sad farewell and heading for the brown river alone.
I watched him fade with the coming of the dawn.

Shadow Boxes

after Joseph Cornell's 'Pharmacy' shadow boxes

Your face reflects across the pharmacy –
twenty vials standing row on row,
a bright shop window filled with alchemy,
miniature magic potions put on show.

Twenty vials standing row on row,
each snugly framed in its allotted space,
miniature magic potions put on show,
enclosed within a small glass-fronted case.

Each snugly framed in its allotted space,
the vials hold a host of time-worn scraps
enclosed within a small glass-fronted case –
beads, a feather, sand, fragments of maps.

The vials hold a host of time-worn scraps –
wrappers from sweets, a butterfly wing, a shell,
beads, a feather, sand, fragments of maps.
In mirror-light, they weave their delicate spell.

Wrappers from sweets, a butterfly wing, a shell,
suffused with fairy tale and nursery rhyme.
In mirror-light they weave their delicate spell –
you see with eyes no longer sealed by time.

Suffused with fairy tale and nursery rhyme,
your face reflects across the pharmacy.
You see with eyes no longer sealed by time
a bright shop window filled with alchemy.

Joseph Cornell in his Brother's Model Train

I love this train. I always sit in the same
compartment where the barred windows cast
faint grids of light across the floor and frame
the shifting phases of the moon. The past
flickers by like scenery, repeating
familiar images, some clear, some blurred –
a palace, sand between my toes, beating
wings, the back of an insect, soft and furred.
I scan the moving world for mystery,
the places where I'll never disembark.
I criss-cross centuries of history,
the burning desert and the frozen dark.
This tiny carriage gives me ample space
to hold the universe in my embrace.

Survivor

after Lighthouse and Two Sailing Ships *by Alfred Wallis*

Dark, unsleeping,
it stands alone, winking
secrets across a restless brown-grey sea.

Its long beam
has pulsed on distant waters,
whitened the frail skeletons of schooners,

flickered over
upturned hulls and waveson,
the battering of bows in jaundiced skies.

It has witnessed
the vain struggle of tugs
pulled under or smashed against the rocks,

the panic of clippers
as they sink and splinter,
their cargo plundered by storm or sudden squall.

Now it broods,
maintains uneasy silence,
as if it were resigned to impotence.

Wrapped in a mist
that can't obscure the past,
it's learning to live with the ebb and flow of ghosts.

waveson — goods that appear floating on the sea after a shipwreck.

The Return

after Edward Hopper's House by the Railroad

You stand in the mist of dusk, mysterious,
your rugged stones worn smooth over years,
weathered, touched by a thousand ghosts.
House of miracle, miseries, memories,
unlocking your door unlocks my childhood.
The air turns cold. I watch and wait.

In the silence spanning our absence I wait,
the bleak moors in the haze mysterious,
fearing to enter you, house of my childhood,
house that was mine for seventeen years.
Do I dare disturb your memories,
break your slumbers, wake your ghosts?

I pause, wary of stirring your ghosts
with the twist of an ancient key. I wait,
till spurred by a starlight surge of memories
rising from crevices, deep, mysterious,
in the darkened air I turn the years
and cross your threshold back to childhood.

I make for the cellars, where all through childhood
I'd go on adventures, looking for ghosts.
My footsteps echo back through the years
down winding stairs of stone. I wait
in shadows, scenting secrets. Mysterious
forms unfold, take shape as memories.

Not clear at first, then clearer, memories
rising like genies from the lamps of childhood –
smells of freshly cut wood, mysterious
crackling from an old boiler, ghosts
in the secret passage, my initials that wait
for me still, faithful through long years.

I breathe your air, dissolve the years.
My footsteps, dulled by sawdust, like memories
by time, shed their chippings. You wait,
assure me each secret is safe, my childhood
intact. Ascending, I feel your ghosts
follow after, protective, mysterious.

I close the door on the years of childhood,
on memories. Wisps of cloud, like ghosts
floating, wait in the dawn, mysterious.

Via Negativa

after Lee Bul's Via Negativa *installation in the Hayward Gallery, July 2018*

inside this maze of lights and fractured mirrors
I know that what I am is what I am not
labyrinthine paths disorientate
every corner leads to another turning
every surface lies   invites more probing
if I look up I see myself look down
if I look down I see myself look up
my body is broken my face reduced to facets
reflections distort what once I took for truth
here I lose my bearings lose myself

here I lose my bearings lose myself
reflections distort what once I took for truth
my body is broken my face reduced to facets
if I look down I see myself look up
if I look up I see myself look down
every surface lies   invites more probing
every corner leads to another turning
labyrinthine paths disorientate
I know that what I am is what I am not
inside this maze of lights and fractured mirrors

Born to be Wild

A Golden Shovel after Emily Dickinson

I craved acceleration's roar because
full-throttle turned me on. Only I
could ride so close to the wind, only I could
lean so low round every bend and not
come off. No blizzard or black ice could stop
my headstrong headlong surge for thrills, my hell-for
-leather turbo skills. I outfoxed death
at every turn, convinced I was faster than he

would ever be and though I didn't take kindly
to the cops, my widow maker stopped
them in their tracks. Speed was what I lived for
– I was borne on air. Nothing could touch me.

The Golden Shovel *is a poetic form devised by Terrance Hayes. The end words of each line in a Golden Shovel poem should, when read vertically, exactly reflect the words from a line or lines taken from another poem, in this case Emily Dickinson's* Because I could not stop for Death – He kindly stopped for me.

The Yearly Trick

The trees are coming into leaf
Like something almost being said;
The recent buds relax and spread,
Their greenness is a kind of grief.

Philip Larkin's The Trees

I walk the graveyard in deep snow,
listening to muffled echoes – the slow
drip drop of water from overhanging
branches, the distant hoot and rattle
of trains, the cawing of a crow
in flight, rasping its leitmotif
across the valley. Though winter bites
the earth and seeks to tighten its hold,
though March is cold and sunlight brief,
the trees are coming into leaf.

The sky, an unrelenting grey,
shrouds what still remains of day
in an impenetrable gloom.
And yet, beneath my feet, something
is shifting, stretching, stirring the clay.
Like Lazarus rising from the dead,
the earth discards its cerements.
New twigs are springing into life,
their green tips arching overhead,
like something almost being said.

Beyond the cemetery gate,
where rows of ancient oaks await
the end of winter, I climb the stile
that leads me back to childhood woods.
I walk its paths, investigate
a snowdrop thrusting its pallid head
through frozen earth, piercing the shroud
of white. Camellias, too, are striving,
beginning to show faint hints of red.
The recent buds relax and spread.

A wind from the antipodes
breathes life into the forest. The trees
are quivering with an age-old song
that speaks of hope and of despair,
of summer's warmth and winter's freeze.
Nothing can shake their firm belief
that all rebirth requires a death.
Deep down they know the ultimate truth –
their finery is all too brief,
their greenness is a kind of grief.

Philip Larkin in the Launderette

The moment I walk in I am aware
that this is not my element. I pause,
then pick my way through bras and women's drawers.
I'm reeling, breathing unfamiliar air.
Piped music in the background – Perry Como –
mingles with smells of wet sheets, steam and Omo.

It isn't like the library in Hull.
I'm used to musty fragrances, old books,
dry air, the dust that lingers in the nooks
and crannies, reverent hushed tones that lull,
not this cacophony of whirr and clatter,
attendants' cries and endless inane chatter.

Yet launderettes are great levellers. I'm lost
for words in here, you might say all at sea,
don't know if I need programme two or three,
which knobs to turn or how much it will cost,
exactly how much powder to put in
or if *quick rinse* is different from *fast spin*.

I finally place my clothes inside the drum
then look around for clues, but with no text,
it's hard to work out what I should do next.
I press a switch – a reassuring hum
informs me there's no mystery left to solve.
Taking a seat, I watch my clothes revolve.

I flick through *Woman*, try to look amused
but let my eyes roam freely round the room.
They rest on cracked uneven lino, foam,
a row of plastic laundry baskets (bruised
from years of kicking) that have lost the art
of carrying and begun to fall apart,

like us, perhaps, who sit here in a row,
each wondering how to wash away the stain,
wash out the deep immeasurable pain
the years bequeath, though secretly we know
all hope is futile, every dream in vain,
our arrows long ago turned into rain.

Present Mirth

What is love? 'tis not hereafter;
Present mirth hath present laughter –
What's to come is still unsure.

Shakespeare's Twelfth Night

This photo shows three girls on a July day –
Feste, Viola and Andrew Aguecheek.
Their final term. Their very last school play.
Ahead of them, the brave new worlds they seek.

Feste brims with joy in her jester's coat,
her eyes alight with laughter. Her stance is bold,
as if she wants to seize life by the throat
and gather up the future's promised gold.

Andrew looks downcast. She stands on her own,
sword in scabbard, blonde hair trailing like weeds
beneath her hat. Intelligence alone
won't be enough, she fears. It's love she needs.

A boyish Viola in red and green
proclaims the power of passion to entrance
and conquer. As yet untouched by 'might-have-been',
she vows to follow poetry and romance.

Now, I look at them with time the only
lens. Viola's dream remains a sham.
Andrew's a professor but still lonely.
Feste drowned herself in the River Cam.

Cursed

'The curse is come upon me,' cried the Lady of Shalott
Alfred, Lord Tennyson

The water's always flowing further,
reflected in my bedroom mirror.
I swam there as a child, remember
how I loved this stretch of river,
the shady trees where I took cover,
the scent of garlic floating over,
free from any hint of terror.

The water's always flowing further,
reflecting shadows of a father.
The smell of breath is coming nearer,
the reek of sweat, his probing finger.
I block the smothering taste of danger,
imagine splashing through the river,
diving in and sinking under.

The water's always flowing further,
reflected in my bedroom mirror.
The gilt-edged rays of sunlight glitter
on surfaces I dare not shatter,
for I am cursed. *Dive deeper, deeper*,
the river whispers like a lover,
let me undo the spell forever.

Trains

Enveloped in a grimy London dusk,
I ride electrified South Eastern tracks
across commuter land, gaze out on blocks
of high-rise flats or soaring towers where bricks
have given way to glass. Graffiti yells
a protest that repeats, repeats for miles
on every wall, inducing a kind of trance.
Lost in the past, I close my eyes and trace

the way the breath of trains festooned my childhood,
soothing my slumbers with a multitude
of low metallic murmurs, rhythmic sighs.
At the slow close of endless summer days,
when sunlight coppered the river, I gazed on scrolls
of steam that hung in the air above the rails,
each disappearing engine leaving puffs
of wavering smoke as wispy epitaphs.

Beneath the cover of my eiderdown,
I chanted Auden's *Night Mail* to the sound
of passing locomotives, their hoots and wails
borne on the wind across the darkened fields.
Soon we'll be gone, soon we'll be gone, the distant
clickety-clack of wheels intoned, their chant
a ground bass interweaving with my own,
our anthem rising to the listening moon.

Ghost Stations

They moulder underground, tracks leading nowhere,
lift shafts sealed or fallen into disrepair.
Grime-encrusted tunnels run across a vast
darkness. Empty platforms shroud themselves in dust.
Preservers of a long-vanished world, they're crypts
entombed in concrete cellars where no life exists.
Down their winding stairwells there's an underworld
of cobwebbed corridors. Glazed tiles still line the walls
and tattered wartime maps remain pinned up, one scrawled
in red to show where *ack-ack* guns have been installed.
Descend. Let them hear the sound of footsteps, the low
murmurs of approaching voices and the slow,
solemn incantation of forgotten names –
Brompton Road, Aldwych, Lords, Down Street, Mark Lane...

Coming of Age

Just eighteen when his youth was lost
as New Year's Eve turned into New Year's Day;
a second warps the future and the past.

He wasn't really driving very fast
but struggling to see through rain and spray;
just eighteen when his youth was lost.

It happened at a place where two roads crossed
and in his headlights everything seemed grey;
a second warps the future and the past.

He braked too hard, too late. The die was cast,
his friend without a seat belt forced to pay;
just eighteen when his youth was lost.

At that age you're too young to count the cost,
and far too young to think about the way
a second warps the future and the past.

One second and the sails fall off the mast;
one second and the stars return to clay.
Just eighteen when his youth was lost;
one second warps the future and the past.

Spring Journey

Scent of bluebells, burning rubber, one wheel
is spinning still. Long spears of meadow grass
invade the shattered windscreen, sharp as the glass
that lacerates my face. Can't move. Can't feel
much pain. Light oozes through branches high
above. A kestrel circles, then resumes
his course. Smells of spring air and petrol fumes
confuse. I shiver in a cloudless sky,
blink at the sun. From every apple bough,
white blossom falls like flakes of snow. The cold
stiffens my limbs, tightens round my chest
and numbs. As darkness comes, I think of how,
beyond the hedge, like runes from a world grown old,
the silent skid marks wait to be assessed.

Vacant Possession

The house has been vacant for a year, he says.
No one wants to live there anymore.
Desperate and prepared to take a chance,
we fix a viewing, drive up after work
on motorways awash with recent storms.

Nearing the town, we wind our way past scrapyards
stacked with mutilated cars, freight yards
crammed with trucks. Galaxies of street lamps
dot the hills; dark mill chimneys, long
abandoned, tower above us, ominous.

At the end of a terrace, an old *For Sale* sign leans
and beckons. We wait inside the car, listening
to sibilants and fricatives of rain
on the roof. The agent comes. We follow
down the hall, like others have before.

The living room is bare, uncarpeted,
the floorboards scrubbed. Only dark stains here
and there betray its secret. A thin string dangles
from a corner, tipped with scraps of balloon.
A waist-high patch of wall is lime-washed over.

We troop to the kitchen, note the horizontal
lines that mark her growing height until
she's eight. Upstairs we pause. This is where
her bedroom must have been. Now, no curtains
conceal her drawings underneath the window,

no bedside rug obscures her etched initials
on the floor. Her scribbles haunt. We sense
that no amount of paint can cleanse the past.
This house is hers alone, sealed with blood
and the remnants of a red balloon.

D-Day

A man puts his watch beneath his pillow
and time dissolves as he sleeps. He follows

the ancient path between the rocks
to the disused well of boyhood. Drawn by its dark,

he clambers down inside the gaping hole
to where the ever-spinning Catherine Wheel

revolves on its pin and sparks fired
from his boots ignite the cobbled yard.

Stars thrive in winter light. They tremble
under the river, winding through hills to tumble

down ghylls and waterfalls. The moon arcs
above an empty swing that hangs from an oak

in a half-forgotten field. It lights the stile
with a rickety step where nettles still grow tall.

The sun rises. A wide sea washes
across his toes. He skims a stone, splashes

his face with water, holds a shell to his ear.
Its drone carries him off in a ship to a far-

away land. The beach explodes, blasting
sand high into the air, its sting

blinding him. A cock crows as he wades
through waist-high fields of poppies, red seaweed

in his hair. The mermaids circle his wreck.
Far off, he hears them singing, calling him back.

One Blue Note

Imagine you can hear
one long blue note
snaking its way
across a late-night bar
and out into the summer dark

winding
down a maze of streets
and rising over purple moors
to a place where the wail
of a distant train
haunts and lulls

opening up a childhood door
past smells of honeysuckle
sticky melting tar
where you see your mother lifting flour
from the cupboard that creaks
your brothers leaning in a hallway
laughing at each other's jokes

follow it round the turn of the stairs
to the bedroom
where you lie with a fever
as the vacuum seethes and whines
where you scribble your dreams
with a squeaky pen
and listen to the nightly symphony of owls

let it lead you slowly
through furrowed fields
of wheat and barley
to the brow of a hill
and a broken stile

float after it
as it fades
meanders through the gloom

rejoins the buzz of conversation
in a crowded room.

Service with a Smile

Clarks
the shoe shop
with the strange machine
that clicked and whirred
and turned my feet fluorescent green
till I could see them shining
through the dark brown leather of my lace-ups,
where mum would watch me wiggle
bright emerald toes
and never failed to marvel at the miracle.

Vallances
the record shop
where many a rainy afternoon
was whiled away
with Connie Francis and Pat Boone,
their disembodied voices drifting through
the holes inside a soundproofed booth
in which my dad and I would settle down
to listen to the latest 45s
and dither over how to spend our half a crown.

Frederick Totty
ladies underwear
for the fuller figure
where Gran went all her life for corsets
and never realised she was getting bigger,
with Frederick dancing his discreet attendance,
unfolding intimate garments
while I watched behind a screen, unseen, unheard,
intrigued by how he glided between ladies,
assessing sizes without uttering a word.

Butterworth's
with sweets
of every colour crammed
in jars on dusty shelves,

a half-hearted bell above a door that slammed
on a heady mix of smells –
peppermint and ginger, snuff and pipe tobacco,
where Grandad lined my palm with a couple of tanners
and we made our way to the till in the corner,
me with Five Boys' Chocolate, him with five Havanas.

Marshall and Snelgrove
exclusive, high class
drapery and department store,
its coat of arms engraved in gold
above the great revolving door
through which we'd venture sometimes as a family,
then huddle together in alien territory,
talking in whispers as we walked the perfumed aisles,
afraid our accent might betray us, or we'd somehow
show our lowly breeding by our nervous smiles.

Those were the days ...

when satchel trailing, every morning
I ran a stick across park railings
and leapt at leaves on the higher branches
of trees or tap-danced over benches,
when I flapped my arms at flocks of pigeons
and hopped the length of the park with flagons
of rum at my belt like Long John Silver
hunting treasure, when every sliver
of floating bark was the wreck of a pirate
ship and I checked my shoulders for parrots,

when I spent long hours pretending to listen
to the rules of spelling or long division
while secretly dreaming of games in the ginnel
with Dennis the Menace or Beryl the Peril,
or longing to be catapulted
out of the classroom window and vaulted
into the field with rabbit burrows,
where I smeared my fingers buttercup yellow,
and safe in the womb of the oak, traced aeons
of time in the fluff of dandelions.

Grandma's Fox Fur

Every winter
it reappeared, as if by magic,
rising like some mythical creature
from the underworld of her wardrobe
to sniff the dank November air.

I'd wait for its re-entry,
wait for the huge mirrored-door
to judder on its hinges,
release intoxicating scents
of seasoned wood and mothballs.

Gnarled fingers parted winter coats,
foraged through hats and scarves,
then, with a sudden flash of fur,
it was there, a writhing snake
dangling from her hands,
its black beads of eyes
fixed in a startled stare.

I'd hold its head against my breast
and run my palm down the deep brown,
wondering how long ago it died
and whether it might somehow
come alive again
if I prayed hard enough.

Every Sunday, I watched her
drape it round her shoulders,
as if it were mink or sable.
There you are, she'd say
to my reflection in the mirror.
Now, is this me or Betty Grable?

Salt's Mill

You rocked me on your knee,
weaving your stories
around its smoke and steam.

Burling and mending, you'd say,
I was burling and mending
from morn till night.

I imagined your ten-hour days
amongst clutter of wool and wastage,
clatter of shuttle and loom.

You spun fantastic yarns
of scouring stones and peggy tubs,
black leading and starched linen.

Now, a lifetime after,
I wait outside the iron gates
that swallowed up your youth.

Unlike you, I don't clock in,
just climb the winding steps
to the ancient textile hall.

Foreign tourists line the walls,
gazing at the latest works by Hockney,
designer kitchen gadgets by Alessi.

Schoolkids, bored with history,
scuffle over badges, key rings, posters,
throw money at the gift-wrapped past.

I stand alone, apart, both feet
rooted to the hard stone flags
where, long ago, you stood.

I'm burling and mending,
the throb of loom and shuttle
pulsing through my blood.

Grandfather's Funeral

I pause on the stairs by the window, glass in hand,
gaze down on the others mourning, recall the tall
white lilies drooping in the funeral parlour
and wonder what you would have made of all

the gloom. Aren't you glad that you're not here?
You were never one for sombre faces,
reverent voices, lyrical andantes.
How far we used to travel in three paces

you and I, walking the windswept moor.
Once, coming home, there was a storm.
You picked me up in your arms and slipped me deep
inside your coat, made me feel as warm

and safe as the elves you sketched, tucked away
in caves in the woods. I think of the yellow kite
we flew on the heath, the Christmas when you cracked
the ice on the pond with a hammer to launch my bright

blue sailing boat, and I'm a child again
laughing, standing on tiptoe to stroke the thick
bristles on your chin. Now, you're as windblown
as the dandelions you helped me pick,

invisible as that ocean room or the house
in the moon you told me stories of and never
tired of repeating. *Just one more time,*
I'd say, believing you would live forever.

Visiting my Grandparents

Anyone we know? she'd call across,
prompting him to read aloud the deaths
in every evening's Telegraph and Argus,
a solemn litany of final breaths
hovering over my homework in the living
room, misting my exercise books, invading
the spaces in between their lines, leaving
me with a lasting sense of something fading.
I can see them still, him with his cigar,
scanning the list to check if long lost friends
might suddenly come to light; her in her chair,
retracing life's beginnings through its ends.
Think on, they'd say to me. *There's nowt like youth.*
The stone they lie beneath proclaims this truth.

Two Towels

Later that summer
they put you in a private room.

Look love, you said,
they've given me two towels –
one for my hands and face
and the other for the rest of me.
Can you imagine it? Two towels!

Dad glanced at me across the bed.
I looked away.
Raindrops patterned the window.
A distant radio announced
the passing of Peter Sellers
and various stars paid tribute.

I'm in the lap of luxury here,
my own T.V. and private bathroom ...

such a different bathroom
from the one at the end of the long ward
where, grabbing my arm,
you suddenly asked,
Do you think I'm going to die?
and I felt my mouth
assume a reassuring smile,
my tongue articulate a flustered lie ...

Fold my towels
and put them by the bed,
then get yourselves off home.

We propped you up on pillows,
left you waiting for the start
of 'Coronation Street'.

There's going to be a death tonight,
you said excitedly,
or so the papers say.

Twin

I venture up, unlock the door and gaze
into your bedroom mirror. Fifty years
dissolve as I press my nose to its surface haze.
Through the mist of breath, your face appears.

The sea of childhood beckons. We trawl the beach,
gathering shells and popping bladderwrack.
Inseparable, we move as one, each
of us the other's half, reflected back.

In August heat, sand between toes, we wade
through marram grass to the water's edge. Turning
round, you tell me to guard your bucket and spade,
then swim away. The sun is blinding. Burning.

I shield my eyes for just a moment, cup
them in my hands as I sit on my heels and wait
for the dazzle to stop. I watch myself look up
and see you're gone. I'm half a century late.

Visiting at Dusk

I make my way
through rows of shadowy figures
hunched in high-backed chairs,
take my place beside you in the corner,
hold your hand and wait.
You stare into a light that is always evening,
wave feebly in the direction of lost years.

I sit in silence, think of storms roaming the skies,
wonder why I never dream of rain.
Sometimes, I watch our past.
Silent as a black ghost
it treads softly over the lawn,
past rose trees, rhododendrons,
tiptoes to the window and looks in.

I see myself a child again
stretched on the floor between your feet
or drifting to sleep
in a room where night lies warm on a wall of shadows.
You stroke my head and sing the song
that asks if I want the moon to play with
the stars to run away with ...

I turn to you and speak but you never answer,
only lean towards me with a grimace,
straining to hear my voice
above the howl of the greying wolf,
make out my half-remembered face
through the dark reeds of lines
that flicker and distort your view.

I kiss you as I leave,
follow the line of your gaze
across the gloom of the garden,
hoping to catch a glimpse of what you see.
Nothing stirs. Only a tired moth
circling a distant light, a slow snail
clambering up a wall at the world's end.

After Summer Rain

The place waits, as it has for centuries,
oblivious of the occasional visitor
searching long-forgotten graves.
I go there after summer rain has quenched
a sultry August heat, listen to the rhythm
of water dripping from heavy leaves.

Insects hover – buzz of dragonfly,
mosquito, hum of probing bee.
Brambles claw my ankles on paths
long overgrown. Tall flowers,
hollyhock high, brush my cheeks,
their petals smooth and furred like velvet.

Drawn by a sudden hint of jasmine,
I make my way to the eastern wall,
its ancient stones still damp and cool
beneath my fingers. They speak to me
of days unmarred by constant noise,
long hours of peace and privacy.

Sometimes they tease, stirring
a boyhood memory almost out of reach –
the musty smell of an old walled garden
with a foxglove closing round my finger
and nettles trailing through gravel,
the pain of stinging hands, grazed knees.

Other memories linger in the dusk,
prompted by the mingled scents
of new mown grass and cypress,
honeysuckle and wild rose.
I follow where they lead, let them
wind me slowly back into the past.

Savouring the silence, I hold my breath,
allow the early evening air to waft across
my face until, at last, I catch the distant
chiming of a church bell calling time.
My white stick picks its way to the home,
crunching a familiar path through pebbles.

Winter Withering

How long have I been clawing at the air,
searching for the way back to a door?
How long has snow been falling on my hair?

Why do restless fingers tug and tear
at starched white linen sheets that make them sore?
How long have I been clawing at the air?

I flounder in an icy sea, aware,
still half-aware, of a receding shore.
How long has snow been falling on my hair?

I press my nose to frosted glass and stare,
stretch out my hands to worlds I can't explore.
How long have I been clawing at the air?

Advancing winter chills – not just out there
but here, within. I feel it more and more.
How long has snow been falling on my hair?

The fog is taking over. Everywhere
I sense a fear I see no reason for.
How long have I been clawing at the air?
How long has snow been falling on my hair?

The Christmas Ghosts

They gather as the light falters
on a winter's afternoon,
moving soundlessy over the lawn
where rust-coloured leaves collect in clusters.

Drawn by the flicker of candles, they hover
close to windows. I catch the scent
of their presence, the trace of a handprint,
a hint of breath as the glass mists over.

Beneath the antlered branches of elms
they linger in the dusk, their voices
rising uninvited, their faces
reflected in the fire's flames.

Their embers burn within, their shadows
haunt. Whenever I deck the fir
with tinsel or light the Christmas star,
I sense them looking over my shoulder,

as if I'm a memory, a link to a past
that stretches back down the ages
across long chains of Christmases
to touch a mystery, not yet lost.

The Pointing Star

Seven Sonnets For Christmas

1. Stardust

We disentangle lights, weave festive spin,
drape tinsel over cracks, festoon the hall
and hope the glitter sticks on every wall,
at least until we let the New Year in.
We straighten out lametta, angel hair,
place hooks through Santa's hat and Blitzen's hoof,
the baubles on our trees all shatterproof,
unlike the fragile hands that put them there.
We spray our window panes with snow and frost,
still longing to restore the spell, turn now
into a Christmas past, a childhood lost,
when ancient stardust fell around our head,
cast from beyond Orion and The Plough,
beyond the oxen lowing in the shed.

2. White Silence

Across the moors, a silence falls in white;
another bitter Christmas Eve has come.
The muffled chapel bell disturbs the night
and summons her again upstairs to numb
a loneliness that spreads through all her years
far out into a sky bereft of stars.
Interred in icy sheets, below her fears,
she burrows deeper than her deepest scars
to fondle warm familiar dark; once more
her fingers touch the sun above her pram,
the golden poker with a lion's paw,
her childhood crib with three kings and a lamb.
As sleep unclasps what memories remain,
the snowflakes gently shroud her window pane.

3. The Magi

Why were they always last? They had a star
to guide them, camels. Every year I'd wait
for them to join the others, twelve days late,
my three kings – Caspar, Melchior, Balthasar.
Caspar came first. I'd tentatively hold
his hand, place him beside the shepherd who
was kneeling down, then hurry to undo
the strings around his velvet bag of gold.
Melchior and Balthasar would bring
more sombre, secret treasures to present,
hidden in caskets made of cedarwood.
Frankincense, myrrh – I'd chant their names and sing
myself to sleep, dreaming of what they meant,
though, from their sound, I think I understood.

4. The Shepherd

The others left at once, having no doubt
about the light, the angel voice. Less sure,
I followed them, not wanting to miss out,
until we reached a partly open door.
Edging inside, I breathed in years of dust
shaken from struts and beams above my head,
caught smells of rotting wood, fresh straw, the rust
on unused tools in an abandoned shed.
A baby's cry proclaimed this was the place
the angels had foretold; the holy birth
was here. I looked around but saw no trace
of heaven. This child was firmly of the earth.
He made me wonder, kneeling at his feet,
can creature and creator ever meet?

5. Country Church in December

No worshipper, but lover of the old,
I traced the path towards the carved oak door;
its latch clicked lightly at my touch before
slow creaking ushered me inside. The gold
of shafted sunlight filled the air and drew
me to the Christmas window of the east
where lion lay with lamb and bird with beast
and time itself was hushed and still. I knew
I was enfolded in a spell. Was this
the artist's skill, I wondered, or the way
history lingers in corners, clings round brass
or sculptured stone? Was it imagined bliss?
Or had I chanced upon a child at play
between interstices of ancient glass?

6. Christmas Eve, King's College Chapel

Why do they come? Is Christmas Eve defined
by flickering candlelight on ancient walls
or choristers' pale faces framed behind
the fretwork filigree of choir stalls?
Do they still expect to be surprised
by stories of a star, a virgin birth,
or in a world now demythologised
is this the closest heaven gets to earth?
The famous opening carol rises high,
the treble solo swells then soars like prayer
beyond the vaulted ceiling to the sky,
dissolving in the clear December air.
Stillness descends, no speech, no sound is heard,
only the candles sputtering the Word.

7. Winter Solstice

Shunning the sun, the axis of the earth
has tilted. Proserpine has gone to ground.
Now ancient myths collect like moths around
our sacred flames, heralding death, rebirth.
In church, white lilies mingle with the red
of holly berries as we congregate
inside its hallowed walls to contemplate
a mystery proclaimed in wine and bread.
Darkness. Silence. Christmas Eve. Maybe,
in the sometimes that is always, the star
of Bethlehem will shine, and by its light
we'll follow Caspar, Melchior, Balthasar,
and see a lonely shepherd on one knee,
and hear a baby crying in the night.

Thirteen Ways of Looking at the Moon

1   Hercules has tossed
      his discus into the dark.

2   A white balloon has lost
      its string and floats alone.

3   A giant snowball rolls above the earth,
      inviting us to come outside and play.

4   Tonight, the eyes are barely visible
      on the bandaged head of Lazarus.

5   Only dreams can be reflected
      in the sky's silver mirror.

6   Someone has taken a huge bite
      from a virgin wedding cake.

7   Who has dared to cut a big hole
      in our blackout curtain?

8   The featureless face of a ghost
      glides by the window, shrouded in mist.

9   Suspended in night's gallery –
      Sliver of Ice on Ebony.

10   From the end of a luminous telescope,
      we're spied on by the gods.

11   Deep in the darkness of the desert,
      a bright oasis beckons.

12   A pale monk abseils over heaven,
      his shaven head bathed in light.

13   The torch of the master hypnotist
      glides unerringly between the stars.

Moonstruck on Blackheath

Midnight. I walk the heath, watch the moon
leak its silver across the sky. The clouds
hover in wavering columns, wispy, white.

Branches of trees bear stars of delicate white
like winter berries, and high above the moon,
Orion tilts his belt at wayward clouds.

Steam from my breath rises in spirals, clouds
the air. A fox scurries beneath the moon,
then pauses, drawn to these misty coils of white

soaring like clouds to the white eye of the moon.

Hymns

They are always with us, substantial ghosts
of church and childhood, steady as an ark
in the rising waters of the seasons,
murmuring harmonies in the moonless dark.

They breathe in shadows, in the dying of words.
Under cover of discord, when nothing holds fast
and the light fails, they rise uninvited
from the common reservoir of our past,

pulsing like a slow heartbeat, restoring
ploughed fields and beasts around a stall,
the sun on every continent and island,
a lone green hill outside a city wall.

Powerful beyond our understanding,
they drift beneath our refuse-laden hours,
whispering hints of a forgotten Eden,
scattering scents of half-remembered flowers.

Oversteps Books Ltd

The Oversteps list includes books by the following poets:

Jean Atkin, R V Bailey, Michael Bayley, Charles Bennett, Denise Bennett, Rebecca Bilkau, Patricia Bishop, Anne Born, Sue Boyle, Melanie Branton, David Broadbridge, Avril Bruton, Maggie Butt, Caroline Carver, Ian Royce Chamberlain, A C Clarke, Ross Cogan, James Cole, Robert Cole, Christopher Cook, Rose Cook, John Daniel, Miriam Darlington, Will Daunt, Sue Davies, Carol DeVaughn, Hilary Elfick, Jan Farquarson, Sally Festing, Rose Flint, Rebecca Gethin, Terry Gifford, Giles Goodland, Cora Greenhill, David Grubb, Charles Hadfield, Oz Hardwick, Ken Head, Bill Headdon, Graham High, Jenny Hockey, Jenny Hope, Doris Hulme, Ann Kelley, Helen Kitson, Wendy Klein, Kathleen Kummer, Marianne Larsen, Patricia Leighton, Genista Lewes, Anne Lewis-Smith, Janet Loverseed, Mary Maher, Antony Mair, Alwyn Marriage, Marie Marshall, Fokkina McDonnell, Joan McGavin, Denise McSheehy, Andrew Nightingale, Christopher North, Jennie Osborne, Helen Overell, Mandy Pannett, Melanie Penycate, W H Petty, Glen Phillips, Sue Proffitt, Simon Richey, Lynn Roberts, Mary Robinson, Elisabeth Rowe, Ann Segrave, Richard Skinner, Alex Smith, Jane Spiro, Robert Stein, Anne Stewart, Angela Stoner, John Stuart, Paul Surman, Michael Swan, Diane Tang, Susan Taylor, Michael Thomas, John Torrance, Mark Totterdell, James Turner, Anthony Watts, Christine Whittemore and Simon Williams.

For details of all these books, information about Oversteps and up-to-date news, please look at our website and blog:

www.overstepsbooks.com
http://overstepsbooks.wordpress.com